Mattie

A Patchwork Masterpiece

Nelby A. Littleton

ONE11

One11 Publishing
Libertyville, IL 60048

www.one11publishing.com

Publisher: Sedrik Newbern, Newbern Consulting, LLC
Editor: Linda Wolf, Network Typesetting, Inc.
Cover Designer: Scott Ventura, Integraphix, Inc.

Printed in the United States of America
First Edition: October 2018

Author's Note
This book, based on my life experiences, is for learning and teaching purposes only.

ISBN Paperback 978-0-9982892-6-7
ISBN Digital 978-0-9982892-7-4

Library of Congress Registration Number: TX 8-660-200

One11 Publishing is an imprint of
Newbern Consulting, LLC.

Dedication

In Memory of My Grandmother
Mattie Lee (Readus) Binford Evans Brown

My grandmother passed from this life into her eternal rest in 1996, but her heart still beats within me. Through the years of making me what I was to be, Grandmother took the weight and carried it. She carried it on the hot, dusty, graveled roads into the cotton fields and back home at the close of the day. She held the weight of the responsibility of shaping a life tightly in her hands; the same hands used to stir the batter of the cornbread and place it inside the wood-burning stove. In her heart, Ms. Mattie held me and for all of the years of knowing her, my heart is full of her. I am immensely indebted to her for the life she lived. I am charged to live by the life lessons she passed on to me. I honor her as my grandmother. I strive to possess her strength and pass on her legacy. My grandmother will always be my strength, even in death. I am so grateful for her life. I am honored to be her granddaughter. – N.A. Littleton

In Memory of My Brother
Ronnie Evans

You left us much too soon and unexpectedly. God gave us fifty years with you. He blessed you with an infectious smile to light up a room and laughter deep and strong. You suffered the loss of your only son and bore your pain deeply. In your passing, you left two beautiful daughters and two lovely granddaughters to forever carry on the smile, the laughter, and the joy we will greatly miss from you. I am forever thankful to be your little sister.

Table of Contents

Acknowledgments

To the following persons without whom my life would be incomplete, I humbly dedicate this book in hopes the reflective thoughts about my grandmother and the lives she impacted will become as cherished a memory for each of you as it is for me.

To my children: Ashli Nicole Evans Littleton and Jordan Lee Littleton

You are more than an extension of me. Both of you are unique and gifted individuals whom I love with my whole being. I am often spellbound and speechless at the awesomeness of both of you. You managed to successfully maneuver through childhood into adulthood with me as your mother. You not only survived me raising you, but excelled. I am proud to be your mother.

To my mother and father: Edna Lee Evans Hunter and Etoy Jones

You created me from your union. Without both of you, I would never have made an entrance into this world. Without my mother, I would not have had the opportunity and the courage to move forward in life with the determination to be the best I could be. Who you were in your childhood and youth and who you are now, continue to amaze me.

Although I never knew my father, I gained insight into his character and charisma from those who shared stories of him. In his too-early departure, he left a strong legacy; his two little girls. I am honored to be your daughter.

To my sister: Cynthia Denise (Nesia) Jones Davis

You were my Number Ten Tub buddy, chicken chaser, and June bug copilot. We share parents, a brother, and a journey of memories, real or imagined. For the struggles you endured, survived, and the admirable way you excel at life with a quiet grace and a charitable heart, I am humbled to be your sister.

To my friend: Madelaine Johnson

You have been my confidant for more than three decades. I am a better me for our years of unfailing friendship. Thank you for sitting down with me at your kitchen table for countless days and hours of proofreading, correcting, and improving my manuscript. Your only payment was the priceless friendship we have nurtured over the years and wanting my very best to shine through my words. I am in awe of you and cherish you as my "Jonathan."

To my co-traveler in this journey of life: D'Anna Maria Young Gipson

You continue to be my inspiration. Every sojourner needs a traveling companion to discover new paths, confront difficult challenges, prevail against enemies, and forge ahead into unknown destinies. Your love, wisdom, and gentle spirit continue to propel me forward. Because of who you are, I am blessed beyond measure to have you sharing this journey. *Mattie: A Patchwork Masterpiece* grew stronger because your initial review of pages not yet perceived as a manuscript was followed by five simple words, "I want to know more." For wanting more and helping to make it possible to reach deeper and produce more, I am eternally blessed to call you my friend...for greater love has no man than this.

To the countless number of friends and family who shared an opinion, a thought, and an insight, or just read the unfinished manuscript and provided invaluable encouragement, I am eternally appreciative of your contributions. What began as simple thoughts on how I perceived Grandmother and the lives that she touched expanded far beyond my original intent. My friend read it and wanted to know more. I did not think I had more to give, but she motivated me to dig deeper. From the first pen stroke until now, I have been propelled forward to finish the work by many wonderful individuals; both personal and professional. In particular, I wish to acknowledge those professionals who provided technical insight as well as inspiration; D'Anna Gipson, Daphane Muse, Madelaine Johnson, Angela Grant, and Sylvia Page.

I am deeply indebted to Sedrik R. Newbern, president of One11 Publishing, an imprint of Newbern Consulting Group, LLC. All of the efforts involved in moving one's work from manuscript to print would not have been possible without One11 Publishing. Mr. Newbern professionally, efficiently, and effectively guided the process and did so with incredible encouragement, patience, and support.

Nelby A. Littleton

Introduction

Can you imagine a hand-stitched patchwork quilt made of remnants of old articles of clothing of great worth and value held together by a common thread, a patchwork quilt stitched in love, hard work, endurance, determination, and a strong sense of pride?

Out of the rural south, Alabama grew countless generations of strong African-American men and women whose contributions to the Universe can never be fully measured or appreciated. Ms. Mattie was one of those women. *Mattie: A Patchwork Masterpiece* is about the journey of Ms. Mattie and the lives she impacted as seen reflectively through the eyes of her granddaughter. In the author's introspective thoughts, Ms. Mattie is the common thread that connected the family in spite of, or perhaps because of, hardships, grief, and pain. Yet, it was a family also knitted together by experiences that birth hope, joy, faith, and enduring strength.

If you have not discovered your family's patchwork masterpiece, I hope this book will guide you on a journey of recognizing that every family has such a quilt, stitched with a common thread.

Hearth of the Home

My grandmother seemed to me to always have been old. Of course she wasn't. Grandmother's thinning gray and black-peppered hair impersonated age upon her frame, despite her having butter-brown skin that was seemingly wrinkle-free. Good cooking and good eating had left her heavier than she had been when her children were growing up. Seven difficult years of raising three of her grandchildren drew age to her that was not there. Grandmother managed to retain her inner resolve and spiritual convictions in spite of the racial disharmony in the place where she lived, the struggle to shape the lives of those born through the lineage of her flesh and blood, and the strain of long work and hard living.

Likewise, she was an unyielding disciplinarian and when called to task, possessed a strong backhand. Grandmother was my strength, and from sunrise to sunset, back bent by the heaviness of the times and the responsibilities of living, she bore a load only love could carry.

Mattie Lee Readus Binford Evans-Brown was born where the red clay lay like a blanket against the Alabama ground beneath your feet. The pine trees grew taller than the sky and the cotton fields stretched longer than most country roads. Alabama was the Cotton Belt of the South, as were Georgia and Mississippi. No place was like the South and even the southern attitudes bred out of generations of former plantation owners couldn't get any deeper south than Alabama, aiding in creating the black man's nightmare and the colored woman's fear for her children. Racism smoldered, deeply hidden in the beautiful tall pines and underneath the spacious starlit nights. Alabama was still the buckle of the belt of segregation, Jim Crow-ism and all the other -isms colored folks knew too well. Colored was a definition of what you didn't want to be if you wanted to be somebody. George Wallace and others of his caliber, joined by the shadow of former slaveowners, helped to make Alabama the threshold for spreading undeserved hatred. Thus,

Alabama became the spill-bucket for red blood from black veins and the silencer of cries heard through generations of weeping slaves.

For Grandmother, or Ms. Mattie as some were known to call her, Alabama was the place that gave birth to many of her ancestors and so many generations after her. The red clay of Alabama held the graves of her parents, one of her two sons, and her children's daddy. It cradled the vanishing frames of my father and my father's parents. Alabama was Grandmother's itch that couldn't be scratched or satisfied. With all of its components lined up against her and any colored woman like her, living in Alabama irritated her soul and vexed her spirit, but it didn't break her will. In the midst of the deepest south, Ms. Mattie kept going, never missing a step.

The cycle of plantin', choppin', and pickin' cotton lasted longer than most people could tolerate. The children of cotton pickers were thinning. The few remaining pickers were left to carry a heavier load. During the seasons of planting and pulling cotton, I often watched her leave us, her three grandchildren, to go miles away to the fields. Sometimes she was in the back yard just beyond the hog pen. On those days, I would stand with my older sister and see Grandmother in the field with the other pickers. There were days when the three of us were allowed in the fields. I would spread my fingers as wide as possible to wrap them tightly around a fluffy, dirty-white boll of cotton. I would tuck it neatly inside the cotton sack, pulled alongside Grandmother or Granddaddy (Mr. Jack as he was called by my mother and his friends). It was hard work and the rows of cotton seemed endless. Just when I thought I had filled my sack, Granddaddy would come, pick it up to see how heavy it was, then raise his oversized boot and place it inside my cotton sack. When Granddaddy's big boot finished dancing in my sack, it was only half full and I would have to keep picking. I hated Granddaddy's big boot. Ms. Mattie never needed Granddaddy's big boot for her sack. When it was full, there was no room left to pack down the cotton.

In rural Alabama, oftentimes the early mornings would begin with coolness, but as the day progressed the climate would change. During cotton-picking time the heat of the day could become almost unbearable. Even when it was cotton choppin' time, with the weather more agreeable, the mere work itself was enough to draw sweat. Wisdom and time had taught any cotton picker worth their salt to dress for change. Since returning home from the fields was not an option afforded to most cotton pickers, many had learned to put on several layers of clothing and remove them layer by layer as the day grew hotter. This was Grandmother's way, too. By midday, Grandmother would have begun to take off the clothes she had layered on, as did all the other cotton pickers.

In childhood what can seem to be unimpressive events, in reflective adulthood can rise to the level of extraordinary moments that stimulate precious recall. To have watched Grandmother prepare for the daily task of labor in the fields are now such moments. On days we were not permitted to accompany Grandmother and the other cotton pickers to the fields, I would stand at a distance and watch her layer on several clothes for the day. Her dressing routine was familiar to all of us. Only when she was thoroughly dressed would she turn her attention to us. We knew where she was headed and what she expected from us while she was away. Grandmother was not a woman of many words. But when she did speak she spoke her mind and that was all that seemed to matter in the moment. Her calling and her words to us are easily remembered.

"Come here. Don't ya'll leave this house while I'm at the field. I'll be back directly. Ya'll hear?" She directed her gaze to my brother. He was the oldest of the three of us. Although neither of the three of us was older than ten, we knew she meant every word and intended it to apply to each of us. Despite being the youngest, Grandmother expected the same obedience from me as my brother and sister.

"Yes ma'am," we resounded in perfect vocal

harmony as Grandmother was not to be disobeyed.

"Alright now, go back in the house and I'll be back directly."

Grandmother covered her head with a straw hat as she pushed open the screen door and stepped out onto the porch. She spoke a few more instructions to us while carefully stepping off the side of the porch, bypassing the two steps. We often watched in our usual silence as she climbed onto the back of the wagon that came around to load up the cotton pickers.

On the back of that wagon, Grandmother would engage in light conversation with the other riders, in particularly, one of her friends, Ms. Jessie Mae.

"Morning Ms. Mattie. How you this fine morning?" Her friendly voice greeted Grandmother as she selected her spot among them.

"It sure looks like it's gonna to be a hot one today, Ms. Mattie. My, those grandchildren of yours sure are gettin' big. Big enough to leave 'em now, I suppose?"

Ms. Jessie Mae lived up the road about three or four hills over from Grandmother's house. They had known each other for years. They shared a common grief. One of Ms. Jessie Mae's babies had died not long after he was born. Apparently, the midwife was late getting to the house and the baby had come early. Grandmother's firstborn son had died twenty-one months after he came into the world. Everybody thought he had just come down with a bad cold, but it was more than a cold. Grandmother may never have really forgiven herself.

Grandmother, having found a fairly comfortable spot on the back of the wagon, responded to Ms. Jessie Mae's observation about her grandchildren.

"They are getting up to be some size. I suspect it won't be long they'll be in the field with us more." Grandmother spoke softly in thoughtful reflection of us. As the wagon pulled away, she nodded in our direction. That wagon was filled with Grandmother and a raggedy bunch of men and women. These men and women, like

Grandmother, were not nearly as old as they seemed. They were the neighbors that lived a mile or so down the graveled roads. It didn't matter which road or how far. It wasn't the distance or closeness of proximity that made a neighbor; it was that you knew them by name. They were men and women determined to make a living the only way they knew how; with theirs hands, backs, and the sweat of their brow.

Ms. Mattie and the others were not very well-educated people as others in the city may have been. Neither did they waste their time trying to figure out life but just how to live it and, for some, how to survive it. They struggled to make sense out of it as they went along. Many of them worked from sun-up to sun-down to live on land and in houses they did not own and would never own. They pricked their hands on cotton bolls, swatted flies, and wiped raindrops of sweat from their brows to have the necessities of living. The difficult work and endless hours of hard labor was not just for themselves, but for their children. Their continued labor to maintain a home for their family often extended beyond their own children, oftentimes reaching one and sometimes two generations after them. Grandmother's reach went beyond her children and sheltered three of her grandchildren in the hearth of her sharecropper home.

Grandmother's children had done their share of picking and straining at life amid the white fluffs of seeded softness. Cotton-picking life was a harsh master for which they were unwilling to continue to follow. They each worked their way out of the cotton fields, found their end of the row and left. They rested their cotton sacks and their backs, leaving only unwanted memories behind. Except for one of Grandmother's four children; her lastborn daughter left more than memories and her rows of cotton. She left her children. Grandmother picked up her child's children and continued to work the cotton rows her own child left behind. Unlike her daughter, Ms. Mattie had to keep going in order for her child's children to keep going. It was not her duty. It was her doing. It was her decision. It was her destiny.

The cotton field was not a welcoming friend. If anything, it was an enemy to be conquered not just one day, but day after day. It did not give up its harvest of cotton easily. Cotton pickers had to fight the dust, snakes, bugs, and the urge to quit and go home. One row always led to other rows and just like the pickers' work, the rows were long and slow-ending. Burly cotton sacks pulled low the shoulders of those who dragged them and seemed to have a bottomless pit. It seemed the sacks were never full enough. Like the rest, Grandmother only stopped tugging her sack long enough to wipe sweat from her eyes, get a drink of water, and start again.

Back inside the small, wooden framed house, filled with the presence of Grandmother and all of her ways, I would wait for her return. While waiting, I envisioned her in her big straw hat, overdressed in worn clothes, tattered stringless shoes, and wearing at least two or three pairs of socks which drooped around her ankles. I imagined her reaching for strength to pull and pack another boll of cotton. As the sun began to rise, climbing higher into the sky, it was reasonable to draw an image of her having removed a layer of clothing as the sun beamed down on her straw hat, tossing them in the back of the wagon and returning back to the labor she had come to know as an inevitable part of her life. Undoubtedly, as they walked, they worked to an unheard beat inside each of them. Without a glance to anyone, they followed a common rhythm and held their own until pickin' came to an end.

In the years to come when the vision of Grandmother and the cotton fields of Alabama would become an impressive memory, I often thought of her laboring in the heat of the day, dragging cotton-filled sacks behind her, but I never understood why she did it. The picking and pulling at life didn't seem worth the sweat. We had little money and no running water. We relieved ourselves in a hole in the ground, hidden by a hand made shelter barely allowing enough sunlight to pierce through the slits between the boards. We walked a path we made through the weeds and high grass, winding our way from the farmhouse to the outhouse in an attempt to do all that had to be done before night fell. Fear of frogs, crickets, and snakes kept even the boldest of us off the trail at night.

In spite of her hard work, we still played in a grassless yard dressed in home sewn dresses, hand-me-down pants, and no shoes. Mostly, no shoes were by choice because the warm dust beneath running feet felt like a midsummer's rain shower on a really hot day. It felt good. At the time, I didn't understand the reasons that propelled Grandmother from the comforts of that framed house into the heat of the cotton fields and I really didn't try.

In spite of the toughness to plant, chop, and pick cotton and struggle to make a life for herself and for us, Ms. Mattie remained in possession of her gentleness, and her butter-brown hands retained their smoothness. At the closing of the day, I looked for them to pull the handle of the screen door and find their way inside the house. They always did. When the day ended, Grandmother fed us well, made us wash the day's dirt off our bodies, and thanked the good Lord for giving her strength for another day. Only then would Grandmother lie down on her patchwork quilt, carefully placed on the hard, wooden floor, and fall off to sleep. Morning would come soon enough.

Smells of Morning

Night eased into morning and Ms. Mattie's wisdom had taught her well; don't let time catch you sleeping, or the day will pass you by. About the time the rooster would begin to crow, Grandmother had already gathered the wood, put it in the wide, black, wood-burning stove and lit the fire. The room smelled of burning wood, coffee, and bacon. Time seemed to have stopped in a place far back, and that little house was filled with all the wonderful smells of breakfast and family. It was a warm and a cold place to be, even at dawn.

Grandmother's voice followed the contour of that little four-room house, "Ya'll, come to the table. Food's ready." Her firm commands compelled four small feet to get out from under the comfort of her big bed and one of her warm quilts, touch the wooden floor, turn to the too-tall bed and pull the quilt up over the oversized pillows. My sister and I followed the smell of food and the sound of Grandmother's echo. As we passed our big brother asleep in the front room between Grandmother's room and Granddaddy's room, we found our place at the table and sat down. Bent over the heat rising from the wood-burning stove was Grandmother; her head only a few inches from the ceiling. She wasn't tall. The ceiling was low. She was fully dressed, wearing the dress she had carefully sewn by hand so many years ago. It was fading, but it still spoke of personality and strength that time couldn't take.

All of the clothing was kept clean by handwashing on the scrub board and then putting the clothes in the big faded round washing machine with the wringer on top. The washing machine was brought out onto the front porch on wash day. Grandmother would pull the clothes through the wringer and then hang them on the line to dry. She kept in step, row by row, to music played somewhere inside her head as she wrung out sheets, Granddaddy's big overalls, our clothes, and other sorts of things. The clothespins clipped to her apron or perched between her lips (which also held the snuff between her bottom lip and gums) were then methodically attached to each article of clothing until the line ran out. She would begin again on the next line.

As she arranged the food on the table, Grandmother brushed against the high-back chair as she made her way around us, seated at the table, to the water bucket situated on a no-name place across from the white smoke-stained refrigerator. The wallpaper was peeling and the print difficult to define through years of smoke layered against it. It had been hung over years of other peeling wallpaper and with each peel inflicted upon it, a collage of unknown times and people who had lived in the house formed and made its own kind of art.

The kitchen was warm even with the back door slightly ajar. I felt a rush, but gentle breeze. The air was still damp as the early morning freshness eased through the door. Through open door, I could see Grandmother's homegrown vegetables and greens. Each leaf of the carefully planted collard greens, mustard greens, and everything she had labored to grow, touched the ground from the heaviness of the dew from the previous night's coolness. They lay on rows of dirt piled up to hold them until it was time to pull them. Grandmother thought they would be good for the winter and with the ham at Christmas.

In the distance just beyond the garden, the fence encircled a plot of ground that kept the winter meal; Granddaddy's hogs. They were dirty from their wallow in the mud and none the wiser that their life would be sacrificed to sustain ours. As the weather's change began to signal the coming of winter, Granddaddy would retrieve his shotgun from its sacred place on the wall and head out towards the barn. We knew it was time. In the coolness and quiet of the day, a single shot would ring out in the distance and one of the hogs would fall.

For some, the slaughtering of hogs was the way they kept their families fed. Having hogs could determine the difference between a good winter and a bad one. Trips to town to buy bacon, ham, or other meats that could easily be gotten from hogs were not a common practice. The drive was too long and the money too scarce. Granddaddy kept his hogs well-fed on leftovers to ensure they would keep us all well-fed, especially during the winter when neither Granddaddy nor Grandmother worked the cotton fields. Ms. Mattie would tend to us, the chores of the house and the farm, but Granddaddy would have to find other work. He always did.

Inside the warmth of the house and Grandmother's kitchen, we sat surrounded by the smell of homemade biscuits, bacon, eggs, coffee, and grits. Outside, the rising sun had just begun to show its glory against the sky. The smell of the hogs rushed through the back door, bringing with it a sudden reminder of country living set against the smell of bacon frying in the kitchen. I looked out the door again, and wondered what Grandmother liked about living so deep in the country.

The land lay wide open with few hindrances to roaming, and the people shared a unique closeness even with the nearest neighbor miles down the road. With just the right direction of gentle breeze, you could smell the peaches ripened on the branches, planted just in sight of the blackberries in clusters on the vines. As the colder months approached, it was uncanny the way the birds lined the power wires in the day and the crickets and frogs sang a medley of songs in the night. And on warm summer afternoons with the sound of rain falling on the tin roof, it was almost a spiritual experience. Ms. Mattie would sit in her rocking chair singing quietly as she watched the drops of rain slide down the window and onto the planked porch.

"Hush. Be still." Grandmother would quiet us from our playing. For most, hard falling rain, thunder, and lightning might cause fear, but, in the comfort of Grandmother's house, her quiet rocking and soft humming was soothing.

Seated at the kitchen table with biscuit in hand, I wondered to myself if Grandmother liked living so deep in the South because of the way the sun kissed the sky with gentle rays of midnight-orange and banana-yellow streaks against its face. Or maybe she simply preferred the tall scented pine trees with needles that stuck to your shoeless feet as opposed to the city skyscrapers. The pine trees grew a short distance from the barn. They were magical. They paraded their tall, slender figures before the sunlit morning sky with just a haze of foggy mist to outline their magnificent beauty. In the lay of the land, they had no rivals. Maybe those pine trees seemed a better testimony of the wonder of God's creative power than the city skyscrapers that blocked out the view of the sun in the early morning. Maybe all of those smells, sounds, and sights found in the deep south of Alabama were comfort enough to hold her there in spite of the seemingly endless hardships of living a black woman's life in the rural south.

Was it also possible that the fear of leaving the familiar for unknown places and people also kept her in Alabama? Grandmother may have longed for the slower pace of things and dusty graveled roads instead of paved streets and fast-moving cars and people not knowing your name. I never asked and she never said. The thoughts of whatever kept her there made me smile. Even in the darkness, the sky blanketed with stars was a warm comfort in the night, and her gentle hum when she was sleeping was restful to my soul. It was a good place to be. She was a good place. Whatever kept her kept me, and that was enough.

Grandmother bumped into the kitchen table while sitting down and drew my attention back into the house, away from my wondering and the sights of the outdoors. I was pulled back into the smell of Granddaddy's coffee and his special coffee cup with the little man in the fishing boat imprinted on the side, and back to Grandmother. We were all now gathered for the morning meal. My big brother who had been sleeping on the couch when my sister and I had passed on our way into the kitchen was now up and at the table. No one was allowed to lift a fork until our heads were bowed and prayers of thanksgiving were spoken. "Lord, such as it is, we are thankful. Amen." Grandmother raised her voice only slightly, to make sure not only the Lord heard it, but that we heard it too.

Time would not stand still. Hurriedly it moved, and Grandmother moved. The wagon, filled with the cotton pickers, would come soon. She gathered her lunch in a brown paper bag and headed for the front door. Once out the screened door, Grandmother stood on the planked porch for a moment, spellbound by the freshness of the morning air. The morning had fully come. It eased the sun slightly above the hillside and gently coaxed the moon over to the other side of the sky and behind the hill. The stars that filled the night's country sky with pinholes closed their eyes for the morning and said "Good Day" to the night.

The wagon arrived. The smell of pine trees and coffee was so tranquil that the cotton pickers had to coax Grandmother off the porch. She loaded herself onto the wagon and sat with her legs dangling off the back as it pulled away. Grandmother was wandering out to the fields to get lost in another day of labor. But, Granddaddy was just lost.

Echoes of Silence

Grandmother and Granddaddy share-cropped the land they lived on for the house they lived in. It was hardly worth the work they put in it, but it was home. They, as was common for sharecroppers, shared very little of the profits they worked to make. The simplicity of the way they lived held a rich quality of life seldom found by many. Grandmother had managed to find it and pass it on to us; hard work at an honest living, care of family, and proper treatment of others. However, Granddaddy was a drunk. His simple way of living was working hard and drinking harder. He was a weekend drunk disappearing sometimes from Friday to Sunday night. The gray whiskers on his chin and a few stubbles on his tan face offset his gentle way, and he was around seldom.

Granddaddy wore the shoes of a man, a daddy my brother needed. I did not know I would need him, too. He was the only hope of a father my brother had. His father, like Mother, had found a place to go that could not hold a little boy with him. In his venture for a different kind of life, he had forgotten to find a place that could hold his baby boy. He had forgotten the promises he made to a young woman who had placed her hopes and her dreams in him. When he loved her in the night, the day would not find them together when morning came and their paths took them to different places and different lives.

For a moment, my brother's father and our mother's paths would collide again when Granddaddy eventually left this world. Long after my siblings and I had left the red clay dirt and graveled roads of Alabama, my grandfather's leaving would bring our family back to Alabama. Our brief return would enable my brother to see his father again. But, too many years had passed between them for my brother to embrace him. Even as a young man, my brother's little boy heart could not hold the hurt his father's absence left, and he despised him. His father had failed to be the man a boy needed and now that needy boy was a man—a young man struggling on his own to be a better man than his daddy had been when he wanted a daddy. My brother's father had stayed only a few minutes talking with Grandmother and Mother. As they finished the pleasantries that come with paying one's respect to a grieving family with whom only the past was the connecting thread of the relationship, his father then walked into the kitchen to exit through the back door. As they stood at the door in short conversation with each other, my brother, although a young man, was still that needy little boy longing to know his father. When their conversation ended, my brother had watched his father walk out Ms. Mattie's back door and he would not call to his daddy to come back.

Unlike my brother's father, Granddaddy had stayed. The image of him almost disappearing in his too-big overalls and big boots as he stood at the fence that surrounded the hog pen and watched the sunset still remains. His tall, slender silhouette was outlined against the distant hills. He had worked the cotton fields same as Grandmother and it showed in his slowed walk and hung head. He seemed tired and empty. Life seemed to have left him old and alone in a house filled with children not from any children of his own. He was the man who raised Grandmother's children when their daddy left the world sooner than they wanted.

At the close of his day, Granddaddy would find his way home. Without much to say, he would eat the supper his wife had left on the wood-burning stove, go to his room nestled between the front room and the kitchen and fall off to sleep. In the night, his breathing could be heard from the room as he lay on a bed covered with a quilt his wife had made, but didn't share with him in the night. The morning would come and he would start his day all over again. Until Friday came, his routine was the same; working the cotton fields and whatever other work he found. Fridays would not find him at home or standing at the back fence. Instead, he went away. He never spoke of his wanderings. However, upon his return Sunday night, the scent of alcohol spoke loudly of what he had been doing.

On those rare weekends when he stayed close to the house, often Granddaddy could be found sitting with his chair leaning and straining on two legs against the wooden framed house. The planked porch, like my grandfather, was weatherworn with time. In retrospect, I don't remember him doing anything while sitting there other than just sitting and leaning. With a snuff can in his pocket and his spit can within spitting distance on the porch, he called me "lazy bones" as I wandered past going no place in particular. As I walked by, I caught a swift smell of his dusty overalls and snuff. It was a reminder of hand-cut fishing poles, freshly dug worms in a coffee can that still smelled of coffee—both Granddaddy and the can of worms—and walks with him through the woods to our favorite waterhole.

Fishing with Granddaddy was an adventure, as was the journey to the place my sister and I loved to fish with Granddaddy. The pine trees covered the ground with their long tall shadows as they cast a pattern across the path and made a haven to shield the hot of the sun.

Granddaddy would whistle unknown but fun tunes. My sister and I took turns trying to guess the tunes. We probably got most of them wrong, but Granddaddy would pretend we were right.

Other times he would shake his head and say, "Naw, that's not the right one. Keep trying."

We would laugh and try again.

Granddaddy would tease us, "Ah, you got it that time. Now, it's your turn." Granddaddy knew neither one of us were old enough to whistle. We would push out our lips, point at each other, and try as hard as possible to make the whistling sounds he had made. We would start laughing and Granddaddy would join us.

When we found our favorite fishing spot, Granddaddy began the routine of hooking the line with the wiggling worms my sister, Nesia (Cynthia, her given name) and I dug up before leaving the house and had put in the coffee can. It was our job to fetch them from the coffee can and Granddaddy's job to put them on the fishing line. We cast our lines in the calm water. Nothing else was left to do but lie back against the bank and wait.

If we got weary of the wait, Nesia always started with one question to our grandfather, "Granddaddy, what'cha thinkin' 'bout?" Granddaddy knew the inquisition had begun and he was up for the task.

He would respond, "Well, I was just thinkin' on how good these here fish gonna taste. When we catch some, that is."

"So, you thinkin' we gonna catch some, huh? What if they ain't wantin' to get caught?" She was relentless.

"Don't matter none if they do or if they don't. They gonna get caught. Just you wait and see."

"I think we gonna catch lots of 'em."

"Nesia, stop botherin' Granddaddy so he can concent...contra... well you know what I mean." I couldn't think of the word but I knew she knew I meant for her to stop asking so many questions.

"Now, y'all stop. Y'all gonna chase away the fish." Granddaddy made fish faces at us and we made them back at him and each other.

The fun of fishing wasn't catching fish. It was the time spent with our grandfather and funny fish faces we made at each other. The trip back to the house always wore all of us out, and Granddaddy usually ended up carrying more than the fish and fishing poles back to the house. Once we were back at the house, Grandmother was waiting. The wood-burning stove was heated. Granddaddy leaned the fishing poles against the side of the house as he put down whichever one of us had gotten too tired to walk. He would place the fish on the table and walk out of the house. He headed to the barn only to reappear when the fish were fried and it was time for supper.

"Jack," Grandmother yelled only his name towards the barn from the back door. She knew he understood. Granddaddy had heard and understood as he carried the slop bucket to the hog pen to feed the hogs. His walk back to the house had slowed and the previous laughter in his voice had faded. He suddenly looked tired and strained. With effort, he lifted himself up the two steps at the back door and stepped into the house. He washed his hands in the bowl of well-drawn water, wiped them on his overalls, and sat down to eat. His fish-making face was gone. He had lost his puckered lips which formed the whistling tunes Nesia and I had tried so hard to guess. I looked in his direction, but he never raised his head from his plate. I reasoned the fish must have really tasted good. When he finished, Granddaddy nodded to Ms. Mattie. He pushed his chair from the table, turned, and walked back out the door he had stepped so slowly in.

Granddaddy would never tell Grandmother when he was leaving. He would just leave. He returned home long after Nesia and I had taken our bath in the Number Ten tub and fallen off to sleep.

When the morning would come, and Granddaddy would rise to start his day all over again, it was difficult to figure what life looked like to him. I wondered if it looked any better than it did the night before he went to bed. His hair was thinning. The empty space on the top of his head was an especially fun spot for little fingers to rub and touch with perched lips. Granddaddy covered it with an old hat. The dirty and tattered places on the rim showed it was a hat he had kept for too many years. I reasoned there were many stories under that old hat and in that balding head. However, Granddaddy never told them. He never said much of anything I can remember. He never spoke of his journeys from the warmth of Grandmother's house, his friends, or other family members.

He had spoken of church although he never went except the day of his funeral.

"I just didn't want nobody tellin' me where I'm going if I don't live right." That was all he ever said to Ms. Mattie when she told him the preacher asked about him. Years had passed between catching and eating fish with Granddaddy and the day he died. Mother had come back to Alabama to take us to live with her. Grandmother stayed. Granddaddy left and went to a place from which he could not return. Mother would receive the call. Far away, the telephone rang and

Grandmother's voice on the other end was slightly above a whisper. Her typical, calm demeanor was elusive.

"Edna, it is Jack. He's gone." Mother had grown up with Granddaddy being gone most of the time so she misunderstood and wondered why her mother sounded disturbed.

After a brief pause, Mother asked, "Gone...what do you mean he's gone? Is everything all right? Where did Mr. Jack go?"

Grandmother recovered her composure, "Edna, Jack passed away this morning."

I cried. I loved him. It was Grandmother's voice that filled the house even when she wasn't there, but it was Granddaddy's absence that filled the emptiness when everyone else was home. Once Granddaddy left, although I was no longer in Grandmother's house, the knowledge he was no longer in Grandmother's house either made the nights seem longer and mornings seem slower coming.

Granddaddy had finally made his way to church. A somber, slim stranger had replaced his overalls with a dark suit and gray shirt. Someone had shaved his few gray whiskers and put a tie around his neck. Sunday morning church service transformed to receive mourners. They had come from miles around to fill the little one-room church. On the program was a name I never knew belonged to him—William McKinley Brown. The church filled with people I never knew were known to him. The windows were raised high and fans were passed to everyone who couldn't take the stuffiness of the overcrowded tiny church.

A slight breeze rustled in the trees beside the windows, and I missed my brother. His absence spoke so loudly his depth of grief. On a day that Grandmother would have to let go, her children would have to say goodnight to a second father, and her grandchildren would weep with quietness for the loss of another grandfather, my brother had disappeared into the woods to have a moment of solitude and to say goodbye to Granddaddy. Mother wondered where he was. But Grandmother said, "Let him be, he'll show up when he's ready." Just as she did when

Granddaddy would disappear, she didn't seem to worry.

In life, Granddaddy was a stranger, but in my heart he was the only grandfather I had ever known. He was a man I would come to understand better in death than I did in our lifetime together. He appeared as quiet in death as he had been in life. But, for me he wasn't silent. In the still of that little church, his silence echoed and I could hear what he had never spoken; living fills time with much to do, but death leaves life with too much unsaid. As his head rested upon the white satin pillow, I began to understand the strength he found in just sittin' and spittin'.

The memory of him told of hard work and easy nights. They spoke of unseen joys and hidden sorrows he kept to himself. Whatever in life had taken him from the bed of his wife, sent him into the weekend away from the warmth of their house and kept his words deep within him— all of that was no longer a part of him. His cry of peace was finally heard from somewhere outside of the man lying in a dark suit against white ruffles.

Grandmother sat quietly. She had come to say farewell a second time to a second man she had wed. She remembered the first time she met him and tried to reconnect to the reason she had accepted his proposal of marriage. He had proven to be a good man in most ways, but he lost his fight with the bottle. It had cost them more than the price of Jack Daniel whiskey and eventually it had taken away his life.

She recalled the doctor's warning, "Ms. Mattie, he's got to stop drinking or it will kill him." She had tried to convey the seriousness of it to her husband, but brief nods and enigmatic grunts were his only response. The doctor was only partially right. His efforts to stop drinking had proven more strain than his old and abused body could stand. The coming of his end had been years in the making and there was no changing his course, even when he wanted to do so.

As was his habit, he had staggered in one morning and found his familiar empty bed and fell full force down on the feather stuffed pillow. Sleep had come quickly and Grandmother had heard his heavy breathing from the front room. She sat in her rocking chair listening to his even rhythm. She barely noticed the change. It was his violent coughing that shook her out of her daydreaming and sent her quickly to his side and then running out the front door to the neighbor's across the road to telephone for help. Town was too far and the ambulance was too late. Mr. Jack had breathed his last breath and Ms. Mattie had sought to recover her own.

As she sat in the crowded church, Grandmother's inner strength and calm determination held her steady as she viewed him from her seat. But pain swelled up inside and she could not hold it down. For only a moment her cry echoed through the church and us. Then she sat. Quiet. I looked down at Granddaddy's silent face and remembered our hand-cut fishing poles, the smell of the coffee can filled with worms, Granddaddy whistling tunes, and the funny fish faces that made me and my sister laugh.

Cost of Leaving

The night lingered. Mother had been gone an awfully long time. At least, as a child, Mother's absence seemed endless and increased the chance that my memory of her, her beauty, and her presence would begin to fade.

Mother was a short, but slightly taller woman than her mother. She was small-framed with sad eyes. Her smile was slightly crooked and her smooth skin reflected her mother's. However, unlike her mother, there had not been enough in the South to hold her or keep her working in the cotton fields of Alabama. Whatever her reasons for leaving home the first time, they took her away from the cotton fields. Mother would eventually find her way out of Alabama.

On the day she finally left her mother's home and Alabama, Grandmother had stood on the porch with hope and fear invading her heart. Ms. Mattie thought of her youngest daughter with sadness and wondered why she had not been able to shelter her from the desire to make this journey alone. Mother had not yet borne her children into existence. She left miles of graveled roads that disappeared behind her as paved streets of another state and city drew near. As the dust rose and settled against the sparse blades of grass on the front yard, Grandmother remained for a moment on the front porch. In a brief moment of solitude, Ms. Mattie had spoken with quietness, "Lord, you know best for your children. I know she got her reasons for leaving and I ain't 'bout to change her mind. So I'm asking you, look kindly on her as she goes her way. And, if it be your will, let her come home again." Having spoken from the depths of her heart, she whispered a soft "Amen."

The evening sun faded fast and time called for the night. Grandmother turned, pulled the handle of the screen door with trembling hands, and facing an empty house, she walked into the front room, dropped into her rocking chair, and closed her eyes.

Mother found her place in a new state and city. Nashville, Tennessee was different from the country roads and sharecropper houses with outhouses in the back and cotton fields in the distance. There was no sound of roosters crowing at sunrise or the sight of stars pushing pinholes in the sky at sunset. In her unfamiliar surroundings, she faintly heard her mother's parting wisdom.

"Edna, the city ain't like down home. Folks there ain't likely to take to you like they do here. Be polite, but don't let' em get too friendly with you until you get to know 'em better. Remember how things are. Where you going may not be Alabama, but it's still the South."

Mother heard and knew what she meant. The color line ran the gamut of the southern states. Racism reached far beyond Alabama's state line. Like Alabama, Tennessee had not escaped the effects of hatred that were solely based on the color of one's skin and the misconception of that individual's inferiority because of their skin tone. This misconception also served in reverse to allow some to have a false sense of superiority based simply on skin color.

Nashville, in particular, faced issues of overt segregation in its schools, eating establishments, employment opportunities, churches, communities, and neighborhoods. The depth of such hatred led to instances of violence, denial of seating to eat at certain lunch counters as well as the right to live in whatever neighborhood where one could afford to live. However, Nashville's stance toward overt racism would not go unchecked.

Tennessee State University and Fisk University continued its rich tradition of leadership and produced leaders in many arenas. Students of these two predominantly African-American institutions of higher learning developed leaders who challenged the status quo. They organized demonstrations, Sit-Ins and Freedom Rides. In 1960, their leadership efforts would earn Nashville its place in history as one of the first major southern cities to have desegregated lunch counters.

Nashville was Mother's destination. It was not her Alabama South, but it was the South and it was deeply southern. Despite the climate of racism, it held a rich musical history reaching as far back as the 1800s. The first tour around the world was by Fisk University's Fisk Jubilee Singers. Nashville embraced music and would become well known as Music City, USA. This would include, but not exclusively, Country music with the southern sounds of guitars, tawny voices, and songs.

People would come from all over seeking fame in the music industry. This, however, was not the reason for Mother's journey. At the time of her coming, she simply wanted out of the cotton fields of Alabama and an opportunity to become more than what rural country living would allow. Mother had come before the seasonal change when the autumn season would rush in and be reflected in the changing of the leaves. The trees would become a rainbow of yellows, greens, reds, purples, and oranges.

In a few months, October in Nashville would prove to be a spectacular view. Yet, Mother felt herself afraid and lost in such a beautiful place. It was good that she had known of people who were willing to have her come and stay. She had traveled alone from the cotton fields of Alabama but had arrived to a safe haven of family. She would not be alone for long.

All too soon the city sounds would change to embrace the echoes of a woman in pain while struggling to bring into the world a screaming, red-faced little boy. Mother had no way of knowing her labor pains would not be the only pains his birth would bring. Fifty years later, her same little boy, Ronnie, would be laid to rest as his life would quietly slip away in the same place in which he had come into the world.

Against the stillness of the sterile room, a friend held her hand as she lay inside the white-walled place, cradling in her arms her first and only born son. She had borne him into the world without Grandmother to comfort her and without the assurance of his father. Where had he gone, the father of her child? Ronnie's father loved Ms. Mattie's daughter in the night but lost sight of her when the morning came.

As she looked out the window with her newborn baby boy in her arms into a world she was not quite ready to face, Edna remembered the little wooden frame house, Grandmother frying bacon, Granddaddy's consistent absence, and she longed for the smell of pine trees and graveled roads. Eventually, the call of Alabama and the country homes of her generation and generations before her would stretch to the city and pull her back.

Mother would return to her home of Alabama with her baby boy, but the yearnings from the childhood remembrances that called her home would not be enough to keep her there. However, Alabama held her long enough to find a new romance in an old friend. Ms. Mattie knew him and his parents. He was young, and he was a wanderer. He had found his way to her daughter.

Grandmother often sat at the kitchen table with him as he talked on and on about hoping and wishing for something better than what he had. Nevertheless, he had assured Grandmother he would be good to her daughter. Mother believed his words, accompanied by a gentle smile and a handsome face. Hand in hand, they stood together before the preacher and declared their undying love for one another. It lasted long enough.

When night had fallen still, the cries of a woman would be heard in the tall pines and against the sounds of the crickets outside the windows; a child was fighting its way into the world just as the girl child before her had done less than a year before. Lying inside a room in their house with peeling wallpaper and linoleum-covered floors, Mother pushed hard against the pain until finally the midwife lifted out from under the stained sheet another life that found its way into the South; I was Mother's lastborn child.

The passing of days would turn into years. The responsibility of two babies, a toddler, and two absent fathers would be more than Mother could bear. She had borne the pain of birthing babies and taking care of them while trying to hold on to a wanderer. It was not possible. Her husband had been taken away and locked in a jail cell.

Mother had dreams. The limitations Alabama placed on a black mother with three little ones to feed, clothe, and shelter made realizing those dreams nearly impossible. Alabama could not hold her any longer. She had untied the ties that bound her to her children's fathers, and there seemed to be nothing left to keep her in a falling-down house and no way to make a decent living. Just to be able to live decently with her children and make a home for her family, Mother would have to look elsewhere.

For a second time, Nashville would become her place. Tackling the task ahead of her would be too difficult with a little boy tagging along after her and two babies in her arms. To reshape her life and answer the call of her dreams, Mother decided to leave her little boy. There was a choice to be made and Mother had made it in spite of the pain that filled her heart. Grandmother agreed. Mother would carry her girls with her to find a way and a place for the three of us because we were too young and too much for Grandmother to handle. Our time and place together with Mother would not last. A return trip home to see her younger brother home from the military would end the sharing of our home and a significant portion of our lives with Mother.

Mother would have to make another heartbreaking decision when it was time for her to return to Nashville. It had been difficult to press forward toward her hopes of a life with all three of her children and at the same time take advantage of the education Vanderbilt's nursing program could offer her. Mother would yield, rather reluctantly to her mother's pleas.

"Please let them stay here with me. You go on back and finish your training. They'll be alright." Grandmother had been encouraging and convincing.

Mother had no way of knowing time would creep in and take away so many years so quickly and cloud at least one of her children's memories of her before she returned. She could not have known her absence could change the cheerful personality of her little boy to a quiet, lonely little boy who knew his mother was not there, but could not begin to fathom the reasons.

The night before her daughter was to leave her mother's home and leave her children behind; Ms. Mattie stood at the foot of the big bed and watched her grandchildren sleeping. She pulled the covers and tucked them in under the mattress. Edna had stayed in the other room, seated by the dimly lit lantern placed on the table. Her thoughts were far from her. She knew daylight would soon ease in and she would leave. She searched her mind for other possibilities although she knew it was already decided.

Mother was facing a future without her children and without the warmth and secure home of her mother. Grandmother had slipped away from her observation of us and she stepped into the open space of the front room.

"Edna, it's best you go to bed now, morning be coming soon, and you'll need to head out early." Grandmother spoke in a low soft tone to avoid awakening us and to give some sense of comfort to her daughter.

She had tried to give strength and hope to her youngest daughter, just as she had her two oldest daughters when they made their journey out of their mother's home and out of Alabama. She could only pray, as she had quietly done before. Ms. Mattie ached at the thought of her child leaving again, even for good reasons, but no words escaped her lips. Her daughter would need all of her steadiness to walk out the door when morning came. They turned to each other, said goodnight and went their separate ways in hope of rest for the night.

When the morning broke into the stillness of the house, Grandmother was already up and had placed some food in the familiar brown bag for the trip. Mother found her way into the kitchen. She stood only a few inches taller than her mother. She reached around her and picked up the bag. Mother spoke softly, "Thank you, I guess I'd better get going before they wake up."

Edna retraced her steps back through the house, past the room where we were asleep and lingered for only a moment. She turned to her right and walked out the front door. Grandmother followed. On the porch, the view of the brilliant bursts of yellow and orange streaks across the sky gave a sense of hope and sadness; hope for a new beginning and sadness for what was ending.

In the brilliance of that moment, while we slept, Mother left. She drove down the graveled road to the stop sign where the paved road crossed its path. She thought for a moment of the night before when her mother had tucked the covers underneath the mattress cradling her three children. It was of some comfort to believe her children would be safe in her mother's hands.

When we awakened to the morning, Mother was gone. We were not old enough to understand her leaving and we were too young to foresee the effects. In the years to come, after Mother would return for us and we would go live with her in Nashville, the cost of her leaving would surface. Our mother had left so much more than her children.

Her children lost the opportunity of knowing what it would have been like if she had not left. Her absence for nearly seven years left at least one of her children unable to create a memory of what it was like to be without her. Perhaps Mother didn't know. Maybe she didn't understand. It seemed the need for a better way of life for all of us had made the decision for her and left her without us. Time had not stayed short enough for her to accomplish her goals and come back sooner than she did. Perhaps she had gotten lost in the changing of her life and hadn't noticed the changing of our lives.

Where was Mother when the butterflies hovered over the mud pies two tiny little hands made outside the back door while Grandmother's singing could be heard in the kitchen as she got supper on the table? What place in life was she looking for that could not keep us by her side as she searched for it? When the fireflies danced in the night arm-in-arm with the stars, Mother was miles gone. She was somewhere sitting in a room that could not hold her children. Instead, we played at Grandmother's feet as she sat and rocked on the front porch.

Mother must not have understood the pain I would feel when I looked back in my memories and would not be able to find her. Circumstances and choices combined had taken Mother from the arms of her children and put her so far back in my memory that there was little memory left.

Unlike having to search for images of Mother, Ms. Mattie's presence filled the house and my memories. She was a presence not soon forgotten. She was a patchwork masterpiece; bits and pieces of the past attached to her but did not keep her from being able to move forward as times and situations demanded. The impact of her existence was deeply woven into the fabric of my life and those other lives that drew near to her. Without trying, she helped to stitch together the lives of her children and her children's children. Grandmother was a bit of everything a woman should be and a painful reminder of what she wasn't; my mother.

However, despite Mother's extended absence and my dwindling memories, there were moments to never be erased. Such moments prevented the mind from creating only a faint image of Mother and allowed her to escape her fading shadow and slip into a rear view of time.

One particular memory managed to remain as consistent as it had from the beginning. As a bright-eyed, yet somewhat sad-eyed little girl, I had lazily walked up the two rickety front steps, opened the broken screen door and stepped into a warm, comfortable little room where the wallpaper was peeling and the room smelled of smoke. As I turned to the right on the faded linoleum floor and walked into the empty space that suddenly filled itself with all of me, Mother stepped into her empty space from her hiding place behind the open door. She was young and beautiful, but also somewhat sad-looking. She smiled, delighted with having surprised her lastborn.

Our shadows cast long forms on the floor and up the wall, somewhat distorting our true shapes. The room was small, the furniture sparse. Clothes were hung on nails on the wall and behind the door. Most of these were clothes Grandmother has sewn by hand with every stitch neatly lined as if sewn on a sewing machine. The bed seemed bigger than the room. The quilt that covered it was patchwork.

These patchwork quilts were hand-stitched by the older women who gathered and pieced together memorable articles of clothing into several quilts. Their works were masterpieces; patchwork quilts of bits and pieces of their torn and tattered lives, leftover remains of the past, and remnants of things no longer needful.

In recall, the setting is clear, but the events of mother and daughter are hazy. Mother was and Mother wasn't. Did we embrace, kiss, or did we just stand in the empty space surrounded by things old and smelly? Did we sit together, hand over hand, talking endlessly of nothing as mothers and daughters sometimes do, or did we just look at one another wanting to reach to each other but not knowing how? Did she talk of how much she loved us and missed us and would soon take us home, or did we only think to speak but found that our words had taken wings of silence and flown away? Intact memories of Mother are unable to survive the passing of time and they are lost in fragments of hope and brief glimpses of reality. There was hope she had come to remain with us or take us away to her home. However, the sad reality was that neither had been her intention.

The visits always ended much too soon and the wait for her coming again much too long. I stood on the front porch with my sister beside me while my brother remained inside the house as Mother drove off, leaving a glitter of dust from the graveled road settling behind her. When she was out of sight and the dust had fallen back to the earth, we stepped inside. Time was passing and night was quickly coming. The sun had settled just beyond our view and the twinkling stars highlighted the darkened sky in a majestic dance recital. Back in the house, as always, comfortable and familiar, Grandmother was in the kitchen.

An Empty Place At The Table

The night was cold. A light snow had begun to fall and slowly laid a thin white blanket across the ground. The Jukebox was playing, but no one was dancing. The once vibrant, finger-snapping and head-bobbing men and women just stood as silent statues filled with disbelief. All eyes stared at the table. Eyes were wide open with pain and sudden sadness. Their mouths hung open in astonishment. He was lying on the table and it seemed his heart was missing. Only a second ago it was beating. He was laughing. The night was young and so was he.

Only a moment ago, his friend had called his name, "Toy, there's somebody outside to see you, man." A voice in the dimly lit room had yelled out to the man on the dance floor. Etoy Jones was his name, but his friends and family called him Toy. He was a tall, handsome, slender young man with an infectious smile and a restless spirit.

"Man, what you talkin' 'bout? Can't you see I got my hands full? Tell 'em I'll talk to 'em later."

Toy was fully entranced by his beautiful dance partner.

"Alright, Toy. I hear you. I wouldn't let go of that either. Be right back." Leaving, his friend eased out into the darkness to relay the message to the men waiting inside the car.

Toy and his friend had been good friends a long time and had spent many nights with each other at the juke joint. Laughing and dancing at the juke joint was always refreshing after a hard day of working. Toy always seemed able to talk his friend into taking some of his workload so he could take the extra time to sneak off and place bets or to collect on bets made the day before.

Toy's friend had slipped back into the juke joint, seemingly in a big hurry, yet not wanting to draw attention. "Toy, I think you better go see what those fellows want. They ain't taking it too good you not comin' out."

Toy was hesitant to leave the arms of the woman he was dancing with, but the unsteadiness of his friend's voice urged him away.

"Alright, alright," he responded impatiently

to his friend. Turning to the soft sweetness he was holding, Toy slipped her a quick kiss on the cheek as he assured her he would be right back in her arms.

"I'll go take care of this right quick. Hold my spot for me, sugar. This won't take long."

She smiled and continued to sway to the seductive riffs of the music and the soulful voice whispering sweet lyrics of love. She eased out her words, "No problem you sweet, tall drink of water. You know your spot's safe wit me. I ain't got's nobody else in mind but you. Hurry back. Don't keep me waitin' too long."

Her eyes followed his slender figure as he walked past the tables and chairs randomly placed in the small room and glided easily past the other dancers. The slow, soulful rhythmic sound she had danced to while intertwined with him transitioned to a fast, upbeat rhythm. She watched with a slow smile forming across her face until he and his friend were no longer in view.

Near the open door, Toy spoke with some agitation as he moved to leave through the door,

"Hey, man where those guys wantin' to see me in such a big hurry and all? I got to get back in there before somebody else step to my girl. They're playin' my kinda beat. You know. The kind that makes your feet tap, your hips swing, and makes you act like you done lost your mind."

When Toy turned to hear his friend's response, his friend had stopped at the open door and pointed to a man standing outside under the lamplight with a cigarette in his hand. As Toy approached the lamplight, the man gestured toward a car. "They're over there in that black Caddie. See 'em?" Toy recognized the Caddie, and moved forward for a closer look to see why someone would demand he come out and see them.

The voices in the juke joint had become louder along with the heightened loudness of the music. An unfamiliar sound outside echoed through the night. Less than a second later, Toy had fallen. The force of the sound shook the ground beneath him and rattled the windows of the car. A double-barreled shotgun from a hidden face in the back seat took a man's life as he smiled and leaned forward through the car window. The hidden figure of a face, unknowingly or uncaringly, left two little babies without a daddy.

Tracks were left in the snow-covered gravel from the car speeding away. Toy lay there, still, unaware. The night grew darker as his blood flowed and stained the newly fallen blanket of snow.

"Toy, get up! Get up, Toy! Get up!" He couldn't hear them. He couldn't see the faces of the people gathered around. From inside the juke joint, someone caught hold of his friend's shirt sleeve, pulled him towards the door and yelled in his ear, "Hurry up man...its Toy. He's down. Hurry up...come on." They rushed for the door only to see a handful of men had already gathered his friend's bloodstained body in their arms and were making their way to a table.

"Get some towels.... somebody do somethin'. This is bad. This is really bad. Toy?!!! Toy?!!!" The room was in shock and no one seemed able to move.

The woman he had danced with and who had been dancing with him many nights before cradled him in her arms, unaware of the crimson flood from his chest and back. She leaned forward to search for any hope of breath still within him. "Turn off the music! Turn it off! O' Lord, Toy... why?" But he was gone.

It was too late to rethink his steps. He had made decisions without thinking about his babies at home and their mother alone. Daddy rushed death living life as if it came without consequences. The night he fell was one night out of many nights away from home. If the cold and the snow were not enough to keep him in the house, surely the small faces of his two little girls should have been contentment enough for a daddy to stay home. However, it was not enough for a man who found his way to death much sooner than he had to and much sooner than his little girls needed.

I miss my daddy. Silence broke in. The pain was unbearable and the anger unquenchable. It was a senseless waste of a needed life. A life with less living done than living left to be done. He was too young to die. We were too young. He left nothing. Death stole his part of me and left my heart to beat without a hand to touch it and comfort it in the night when a small child becomes frightened. He should have lived long enough to leave a memory.

Yet, somehow, I felt I knew him. I could see the glide he had in his walk and feel the touch of his hand. I heard the way his voice thundered when he laughed and imagined the sadness of his eyes and the lines that formed across his forehead when he smiled, or the tightness of his jaw when he was thinking hard on something. I hoped his brown eyes softened at the sight of me. In my dreams I saw the back of him seated at the café table. He turned slightly, looked out the window at me, smiled, and turned back to those laughing with him. I awakened and tried to recall his face. But, he slowly disappeared. I cried.

Like Mother, cotton pickin' had become a way of life for him he could no longer stand.

Unlike Mother, he had stayed in Alabama. It was all he knew and all he wanted to know. Getting paid low wages for the cotton he picked would not be his only money maker. He placed his bets in the night and picked his cotton in the day. Whatever the wager a bet was made on, it was worth the sweat of the work to make the money to play the money.

When the weather grew cold and cotton picking was over, Daddy still did not find rest at home with us. A restless spirit and a misguided sense of right and wrong caused him time in the cool of a lonely jail cell. Even a jail cell and his wife having left him while he was locked away was not enough pain to keep him from the jukebox's music when the cell doors opened and he walked out. When night would come, Daddy would leave to go dance to the music played at the juke joint. It was tantalizing and inviting. I was too young to know he wasn't home. When he did stay around long enough to be noticed, he might spend time sittin' and talkin' with Ms. Mattie at her kitchen table.

"Ms. Mattie," he fondly called her. "You got the best biscuits in these parts. You going to make me fat, eating your good cooking." He laughed at himself and Ms. Mattie flashed a brief smile.

Ms. Mattie knew he was a smooth talker. Fancy words had gotten him her daughter and given Ms. Mattie two of her daughter's three children. She knew he loved her daughter and their babies, but in his voice she heard a distance he did not intend her to discover. He longed to want what he knew he should want; his family, happiness with his babies, and a desire to stay home. Nevertheless, he was restless, and she knew restlessness could take a man from his family.

Talks with Ms. Mattie about the frailty of his life, and the thought he would not live a long one, was not enough to make him walk a different path. Toy would confess to her, "Ms. Mattie, I don't feel I got long for this world. I mean I know I've done a lot of wrong things in my life and I should be a better man, but it don't feel like I'm goin' to even make it to twenty-five. I do hope to be 'round long enough to straighten my life up like I ought to."

As they sat, the fire would almost go out in the wood-stove and the warmth of the kitchen would began to cool. Sometimes they might talk off and on well into the evening. In between conversations, he would go in and out of the kitchen, nowhere in particular, to stretch his long legs, think hard on what else he might need to say before heading back into the house. Finally, when he had done all the talking and listening he wanted, he got up from the table, touched Ms. Mattie's hand, and left. He would share his thoughts with her only once more just short of his twenty-fifth birthday.

Daddy's freedom from a jail cell, and a woman no longer his wife, led him out into the night to the café and the café table became his cooling board. That fatal night afforded him one more chance to lay down bets, but the last night of picking them up again. He danced with death and it would be the last time he held us in his arms. He traded a lifetime of future walks in the park, of swing rides and slides, for a dime on the dollar and a pocket full of change. For green paper with faces, he cut short the opportunity for future talks and wiping away tears from hearts broken by fellows too young to appreciate the gentle souls of his making,

Daddy's recklessness for a few hours to stand tall in the eyes of strangers who had become his friends was more important than being around to spend time teaching his two little girls about life and being there when life was unfair to us. I would need his strong hand to ease the misery of growing up and to push me to reach beyond the mistakes of life and to encourage me never to settle for anything less than the best in myself. My sister would also yearn for his presence and affections. She was his firstborn. She would need him to let her know he loved her.

I would have loved to love him. Daddy went away when he didn't have to go, leaving an empty place at the table. How I miss my daddy. His hands are not able to wipe away falling tears. He should embrace our sweetness wrapped in his own flesh and blood, but never will. Instead, his hands were folded across his chest as he slept. Let me awaken him!

The music softened to a slow and mournful sound, barely audible above the wails of the mourners. Small and unsure of all that was going on in the crowded, perfume-filled room, I turned in search of my mother. However, Mother was not there. The deeply fallen snow and harsh winds kept her out of Alabama and out of my reach. I searched to see my daddy, but tall black trees surrounded the light and weeping willows draped in clothes of sadness and pain hid him from my view. Their pain was for themselves and for us, his little girls. Drops of rain fell on my face; salty and warm. Black, beautiful trees bent low. Their grief was increasingly intense and more than they could contain. The rain poured, and the droplets shattered against the softness and hit the floor.

They hid their faces behind veils of sorrow as they came slower and closer to see him. They had come to let him go. My small hands reached down from Grandmother's arms to touch his face, but she pulled back and he was out of my reach.

Ms. Mattie spoke no words. Only tears eased from her eyes and she remembered their talks in the warmth of her kitchen. He had called her "Ms. Mattie" for longer than she could remember. Even when he grew into a man and sought out her youngest daughter for his wife, he still called her Ms. Mattie. She knew he had not been raised with his own father or his mother; death had taken them from him early in his life. Growing up had not been pleasant for him, his brothers, or his sister. After the death of their parents and separation from each other, some family members had not been kind to all of them. Some of his siblings were treated better than the others depending on which family members took on the responsibility to raise them. Toy had his older sister to watch out for him, but neither of them was old enough to ward off the nastiness of some family members. They often found themselves without enough food for the both of them. His older sister would ensure he had enough to eat even if she did not. She was his protector. She loved him. But, even she was not enough to shelter him from his own adult choices and ensure he had a long life.

Ms. Mattie flashed back to the night his last baby girl was born. Toy had waited outside of the house in the August heat, pacing, drinking, and humming a non-distinctive tune. A cry broke though the silence and the midwife called to him, "You got yourself another little girl. Come on in here and see for yourself." He was just as proud as he had been with his first baby girl. Ms. Mattie had seen the look of pride on his face when he entered the room, almost toppling over the chair next to the bed. It was a night to remember.

Drawn back to the overstuffed church and wailing women and men holding their hats in their hands and wiping their eyes on the backside of the sleeves of their shirts, Grandmother wanted to forget. She wanted to forget his words, "Ms. Mattie, it don't feel like I'm goin' to even make it out of my twenties." Perhaps, she thought she should have warned him to follow his first mind and told him, "Toy, you might be right so you need to start changin' the way you livin'. Now, you know I'll be here if anythin' should ever happen. But those babies need you."

The moment had slipped away and she could not change the outcome of his choices. Ms. Mattie wanted to forget the night he fell and his baby girls lost their daddy. She wanted to forget the word that came to her front door that another colored man had been shot down for no good reason by no-good people. Ms. Mattie knew the South could be a dangerous place for any colored person—man or woman. She also knew it was not always at the hands of Southern white men who despised a colored person for just being colored. There were all kinds of meanness in the world. To keep company with the wrong type of people or to make the wrong choices could end a man's life just as easily as the rope from a lynching.

The preacher offered words of comfort from the worn-out Bible from which he had been reading. He struggled to find the words that would comfort, but also warn the living of the consequences of their choices. By the presence of all in attendance, he could see their love and their great grief at the senseless death of this very young father. While he did not want to enlarge their hurt and their pain by recalling the reason death had come so soon in this young man's life, he felt it his spiritual duty to ensure if any other young men were heading towards the same destiny, they understood there was still time to alter the course of their lives.

Having ended what he hoped would honor the fallen and warn the living, the preacher nodded to the funeral directors to come forward. This indicated to everyone it was time for everybody to stand while the funeral directors got ready to roll my daddy out of the church. I held a little tighter to Grandmother and watched as the top closed and my daddy disappeared.

Number Ten Wash Tub

The kettle's whistle sounded to signal the water was hot and ready for Grandmother to pour into the big round Number Ten washtub. Grandmother summoned two very dirty little girls to the room where the tub had been filled. The tub seemed small compared to Granddaddy's room. His room was the closest to the warmth of the kitchen to take baths when it was cold. The room was comfortable with little in it; a too-tall bed covered with one of Grandmother's quilts and a pair of old boots in the corner. Granddaddy's shotgun was mounted on the wall, temptingly placed, but forbidden to touch.

When the door was slightly ajar, a slither of light from the front room could be reflected off the galvanized siding of the Number Ten tub. However small, the Number Ten was big enough to hold two small little girls at bath time. My sister and I did more playing and splashing in that Number Ten tub than washing. The wooden floor of Granddaddy's room always took more of a washing than the two of us as a soapy stream of dirty brown water would spill out on the floor, seep between the planks, and form a small puddle underneath the house.

In the Number Ten, my sister and I were full of laughter at the way we had played with the grasshoppers and pretended they were chickens while pulling their legs off and pretending to cook them in the lid of a jar of Vaseline. The Number Ten brought common memories and kept us as happy as we could be without our father and our absent mother.

Our bond was great. We shared the joys of climbing the trees in the front yard, playing with our brother and flying June bugs. There were three types of trees in our front yard and we each had picked our tree. I was the youngest and smallest. The shortest tree was my climbing tree. My brother was the oldest and had the tallest and biggest tree. My sister's was in the middle. Nature had grown those trees three in a row, all varying sizes. They just happened to fit us.

My brother, still just a little boy without his

father and our mother, joined us sometimes catching and flying June bugs. He was the expert at tying the strings on their legs. If it were not done just right, the leg would come off and the June bug would get away. He would leave, however, when we decided to make mud pies or pretend to cook grasshoppers.

As we splashed the water, we talked incessantly about nothing, as sisters often do.

"Hey Nesia, what we gonna do tomorrow, huh?"

Sounding uninterested, Nesia answered, "Don't matter to me. Same thing we did today, I guess." She always said it didn't matter. However, she always had ideas.

"Well, if it don't matter to you, and if Grandmomma lets us, maybe we can go pick plums. You wanna?" I liked picking plums but I really loved eating them on the way back to the house.

"Don't see why not. But we can't eat 'em all this time. Last time Grandmomma got really mad. Remember?"

Looking toward the closed door where Grandmother was nearby, I responded quietly, "How could I forget? She said next time if we do that, she gonna whoop us." I knew Grandmother meant it and I would try harder not to eat them.

My sister, recalling another painful incident, also spoke softly, "Yeah, huh? Like she done that time she thought we went in Sallie's house when she told us not to go in and not to eat at they house. Remember?"

I remembered. Grandmother's discipline with a switch in her strong hands could easily recall to one's mind lessons not to be forgotten.

"Oh yeah, we didn't even go in they old house no way. We was out back looking at them hogs they got. I liked the little baby ones with the patches on 'em"

Nesia laughed, "They was kinda cute and fun to watch, huh? But we still got a whoopin' cause she didn't believe us. Just cause she couldn't see us from across the road didn't mean we went in the house. She could have asked Sallie's momma did we go in the house. But she didn't. She just whooped us."

Nesia frowned at the remembrance of the pain and hurt pride of Grandmother failing to believe our denial, "That wasn't right, huh? I'm sure glad she didn't get hold of us like she did Ronnie when he lost his watch playing in the woods."

I started to chime in, "Me neither. But…" Nesia started to laugh out loud.

I frowned at her, hoping to quiet her, "Shhhh, we gonna get in trouble. Why are you laughing anyways?" I did not want Grandmother to have to pull herself from her evening work to come in and hush us up.

Nesia regained her composure and continued with the story. "Ronnie was funny. He took off running outside the house. He was running 'round the house with Grandmomma chasing after him"

"Oh yeah, right, huh." I interrupted. "He stopped, looked under the house to see where she was, and took off running again. That really was sorta funny. Probably not to him, though." I knew

4

I would not have thought it was funny.

"Yeah, it wasn't funny, though, when she caught up wit him." As Nesia spoke, she wiped her eyes from the water I had accidentally splashed in her face while trying not to laugh too loud.

Feeling a little guilty for laughing, I defended my brother, "She ought not to have whooped him though. He didn't mean to lose it. Besides, he kept those boys from hurtin' us that one time. Remember?"

I was proud of my big brother for that day. We were young, but when Grandmother had to go to the field she left us at home. Ronnie was always in charge.

"Yeah, I remember." Nesia looked a little sad at the thought of that day. "He was really arguing with them big boys to leave. It was two of them, too. They ran off and never came back, neither." The pride in her voice filled the room. We never told Grandmother. It was much more fun staying home than having to go with her and Granddaddy to the cotton field.

We sat still for a moment, remembering how brave we thought our brother had been trying to protect his little sisters from those boys. The boys were brothers and part of a large family that lived in a big, old white house at the end of the same road where we lived. We were not friends with them. Grandmother did not allow us to play at their house, because they were always fighting with their younger brothers and sisters. They were not permitted at our house, either. However, the two boys had come while Grandmother and Granddaddy were in the field, my sister and I were playing on granddaddy's bed and Ronnie was in the kitchen eating.

A thud of the front screen door halted our playing and brought Ronnie out from the kitchen. Like most folks that lived on the graveled roads and knew their neighbors, we did not lock our screened door. The front room of the house was small and had a direct view from Granddaddy's room to the front door, but Nesia and I only caught sight of the boys as they entered the doorway of Granddaddy's room. Both boys were dressed in dirty overalls, tattered shirts and old sneakers with holes in them. Ronnie had stepped between the boys and the bed where Nesia and I were still seated. Surprised by their sudden presence, we had stopped playing but had not moved off the bed.

Ronnie raised his voice in anger at the intrusion of the boys, telling them they had to leave. He and the two boys matched each other's heighten anger and threatening words. When they attempted to move closer into the room and raised their fists towards him, Ronnie took a quick step to his left and made an obvious side glance at the wall. Granddaddy's shotgun was on the wall and Ronnie knew how to use it. He turned back to glare at the two boys who had stopped just a few feet in front of him when he had stepped to his left. If Ronnie was afraid, it was not evident to us and apparently not to the boys. They lowered their voices as they backed away, turned and ran out of the house.

The moment did not last long. We went back to our pointless dialogue and recollections of the day. Our bodies had gathered dirt from crawling on the barn floor to make egg raids on the setting hens. We added even more dirt and sweat from chasing chickens until they refused to run. The fun we had was worth the bath in the Number Ten.

We heard Grandmother's voice from the front room saying that we had been in long enough. We finished washing off the evidence of the fun we had that day and got out of the Number Ten. At the end of the day, the Number Ten was our place of solace to recount the events of the day. Even days that were not as fun and exciting as other days were still made tolerable by the power of the Number Ten washtub. It brought comfort and security. It was our moment of togetherness no one else shared or understood. For Grandmother, it was simply bath time to wash off the dirt of the day. For my brother, it was more time to watch the black and white television without our interruption. Granddaddy was absent.

Outside the window, as we dressed for bed

and crawled underneath the covers, night had encroached on the day. It seemed that the day had just started and it had already grown darker. The pinholes punched in the sky let in a few sparkles of light here and there. You could see for miles into the darkened sky. There were no disruptions of too-tall buildings invading the view or bright city lights fading out the stars. As always, Alabama nights in the country were nights without the unpleasant sounds of city life. No loud cars or horns beeping. Only the musical sounds of frogs and crickets made up the night chorus as a weary and worn-out child's lullaby. It didn't seem to matter that Grandmother's voice from her pallet on the floor urged two tired giggly girls to stop moving and go to sleep. Ms. Mattie had earned her rest on the quilt. Night shut the door and stillness slipped in underneath the covers. The overflow of hard work and harder living, of exhaustion and weight, eased out in a rhythmic sigh as she fell asleep.

The small room, covered with darkness, embraced us as Grandmother rested a body and a mind that had borne years of labor; some for her own sake and some for us. She labored as if we had come through her loins. In the stillness, I listened. She lay with only the upward thrust of her chest, as breath was unconsciously drawn in, and the downward drop, as it was let go. The rhythm of her restfulness and ours went on into the night until the morning crept in and Grandmother rose to wake the sun.

God and Grandmother

The day broke into the night and rolled back the pin-holed blanket from across the sky to kiss the morning. The night chorus was replaced with the heavenly choir of God's songbirds. It was Sunday. Cotton was picked from Monday to Friday. Other work was done on Saturday. However, on Sunday it was time to go to church.

Grandmother had already gotten up from her pallet on the wooden floor and was in the kitchen. The sound of Grandmother in the kitchen and the smell of the food eventually brought two sleepy little girls and one little boy out from underneath the covers to a warm and familiar kitchen. Grandmother moved swiftly around the kitchen. Having done it for years, she knew every obstacle to avoid that might slow her step as she placed the fried eggs, sausages, and biscuits on the table. Granddaddy had also gotten up with the morning, dressed, and found his way to the table. Without much conversation with any of us, Granddaddy ate, finished the last drop of coffee, wiped his mouth with the back of his hand, and nodded a gesture of gratitude to Ms. Mattie before he disappeared out the back door. Granddaddy never went to church.

After breakfast, it was time to get ready for church. Grandmother wasted no time making sure we were properly dressed before she sent us outside. Grandmother would never be late for church and would tolerate no excuses from her grandchildren for any delay. She was always the last dressed, but she was always on time.

Grandmother's voice filled the entire house and the outdoors with a soulful wailing that only comes from years of living and depending on God. The radio was tuned to the 1960s WGOK; a black gospel station physically located in the middle of a swamp in Mobile, but which could be picked up deep in the country. Filled with the longing for a place far from where she was and a hope for something or someone to lift the weight of her existence, Grandmother slowed down only long enough to listen to the songs on the radio, "Someone to share...someone to care...like none other can do. He'll come down from the sky and wipe the tears from your eyes. You're His child and He cares for you."

Somewhere between listening and dressing, Grandmother began to speak aloud words I could not fully comprehend. Tears fell from her face. But, they were not tears of sadness or moaning of pain. In her singing, she must have remembered the blessings of restful nights and the joys of being able to experience the morning sun. It was her way to thank her Creator for letting her live and work another day. Outside, something stirred inside me. I could hear Grandmother and the voice on the radio become lifted out of themselves and carried to a place beyond the present moment they were sharing together. I didn't know what stirred me and why my insides refused to be still. Yet, in the movement was tranquility—a kind of knowing that you can't explain but do not want to lose. Somehow, it had to do with all the stuff going on inside the house with Grandmother and the voice inside the radio. Eventually, she emerged from inside the house, fully dressed and ready to go. We stepped off the soft grass onto the gravel road and began our walk to church.

Church was good. Church was every Sunday and sometimes on Saturday night if a revivalist was in town. No matter which day, the sounds of singing and people shouting "Amen" floated out the raised windows, caught the air and spread like fine mist over the rows and rows of cotton situated along the road that led us to church. It was a one-room, wooden-floor church with hard seats filled with lots of dressed-up women with big hats and men in their Sunday best. The sound made by the feet stomping the floor and voices raised high and loud was warm and sweet. It melted in your ears, eased down into your soul, and became a permanent part of you. Good church always meant good singing, clapping, praying, and preaching.

The walk was long, and the sun was hot. I held my head down and kicked gravel with my shiny black patent-leather shoes as we walked. It was an irritation to Grandmother. A few steps behind, Grandmother gave her usual reprimand,

"Hold your head up! How you know where you are going?" Grandmother was a woman of great pride. Whatever situation she found herself having to endure, she kept her head up. It was not held as one who thought she was better than others, but one who knew she was not less than anyone.

The walk always seemed longer than it was in reality, but familiar landmarks offered some comfort that we were getting closer. Doc's house was one of the most well-known places to everybody who lived in the area. It was big and white. None of the colored folks in the area and none that we knew of even in the city owned houses like Doc's. It sat back off the paved road with its manicured yard and big fine car in the drive. Grandmother never mentioned how spectacular it was, but she always managed a glimpse of it no matter how often we passed it.

The difference between that magnificent landmark and our Aunt Nellie's house was striking. It was as plain as black and white. Aunt Nellie was really great-great-Aunt Nellie but everybody just called her Aunt Nellie. Her house was not as visible from the paved road, although it sat alongside it. The trees had grown too large for the yard and the weeds and grass needed tending. The front of the house faced the front of another smaller shed-like frame where she kept many unrecognizable things. A piano sat just outside her door. No one knew if she ever played it.

It was clear she lived alone and preferred it that way. Grandmother seldom visited her, but when we did, our visits were never long. It seemed Grandmother felt an obligation to drop in every so often. Obligation or no, she never stopped on our way to church. Nothing stopped Ms. Mattie from church and God.

As we drew nearer to the church, Grandmother's steps grew a little lighter than she had walked during the week and moved a little faster. The voices from up ahead seemed to pull her in. Before the beat stopped, kept in time by hard shoes softly tappin' against the hardwood floor, the preacher stood up. His voice was weighty as if he was carrying a burden that was more than his, but for some reason, he wanted to carry it. His words were repeated at the end of a long sentence and then by an "Amen, preach it brother," from the dressed-up women with the big hats. The men stood up, waving their arms over their heads. The children just giggled. None of the reactions of the people stopped that preacher from yelling and spitting. Instead, it seemed their voices lifted him up and out of himself. He stepped on air and walked the rail in front of the pulpit.

It was magical and everybody was caught up. Grandmother yelled something loud and began flinging her arms in the air. Her hat caught the wind and left her head. It landed in another lady's lap, but not for long. Whatever got a hold of Ms. Mattie must have gotten a hold of that lady, too. The preacher's white handkerchief was wet and he was waving it above his head. His veins stood out so far on his neck it looked as if maybe he had swallowed a worm while his mouth was so wide open. Whatever he had swallowed made him sound strange and good all at the same time.

Ms. Mattie retrieved her hat and settled back down on the seat. The soulful music from voices mixed with wailing eased the preacher off the rail and placed him back behind the pulpit. Sweat ran down his face to the tip of his chin and against the white handkerchief he had been waving around. He stretched out his long dark brown arms from underneath his black robe and invited all the sinners to come to Jesus.

"Come children...come on to the Lord. Come children...bring the young 'uns, bring yourselves to Jesus...he's waitin' for you." His invitation to come forward and accept Jesus into their lives was compassionate and filled with all of his convictions.

The gatherers began to sing, "Just as I am without one plea, but that His blood was shed for me..." As their voices lingered in the air, people came. Some, especially children, seemed a little reluctant, as if some force had pulled them forward and dropped them in front of that preacher.

Others came crying, "Lord, save me, Jesus,"

Nelby A. Littleton

and some solemn and tearful, quietly nodding and saying, "Yes sir, preacher, I wanna know the Lord."

Then all the other folks in the seats started clapping and shouting all over again, "Some glad morning when this life is over...I'll fly away..." until finally that preacher raised both of his hands high over everybody, spoke a few words and told us we could all go home. The preacher led us out and waited at the door to thank all of us for coming.

"Ms. Mattie, you sure looking mighty fine this Sunday morning. It's mighty good to see you."

"Thank you. Yessir, Preacher, I'm always prayin' to be able to get to church. I can hardly see making it through the week if the Lord didn't keep giving me strength. You remember my grandchildren, don't you?"

"I most certainly do, Ms. Mattie. These are some fine little girls you got here. Don't you worry none 'bout 'em, either. Just keep raisin' 'em like you doing and they'll come out just fine. I didn't see your grandson. Tell him I want to see him next time we meet. Y'all have a good day now, you hear?"

"Yessir, we surely will." She was somewhat embarrassed the preacher had mentioned my brother's absence. She hid it well and never missed a step in her response, "You do the same. We'll see you next service."

Grandmother gathered us up and began our walk home. As we left the little church behind, the soulful sounds of the music seemed to linger in the air. The preacher's thunderous voice of faith and hope, sin and repentance echoed in my ear and deep down in my soul. The people's weeping at the call to come and give themselves to Jesus was a testimony to the power of Grandmother's God to reshape and reform lives. I wasn't sure what had happened that Sunday or any other Sunday at Grandmother's church. But, whatever it was, I liked it and always looked forward to sitting in that little church with God and Grandmother.

A Different World

Ms. Mattie got up to wake the sun. It had rested during the night just below the foothills. But now, Grandmother had things to do, so the sun would have to get up. From the foot of the pines, it climbed and came to sit on the tip of the tallest one. Having had a full rest, it stretched rays across the sky. Grandmother began each morning waking the sun, then two sleepy little girls and one grumpy boy. It was her daily routine to prepare breakfast and then prepare us for whatever would be the task of the day.

It was near the end of three months from the last time Grandmother bought food from the town store. Whatever food wasn't grown in the soil, grazed on the land or bought off the food truck that came by the house, Grandmother went to town and bought. Grandmother seldom went into town because she did not have transportation. It appeared only the necessity of needing to buy food would bring my Grandmother into the crowded and unfriendly city. It was a different world from where she spent most of her growing up. If there were other reasons, she did not say.

Unlike church on Sunday, town was too far to walk. Grandmother could always rely on an old friend to come and take us. Granddaddy never went with us into town. He never said why, either.

An old, long, dirty, white car pulled up to the house and a big man was seated behind the steering wheel. He didn't bother getting out. The car was close enough to the house for Grandmother to hear him blow the horn. However, there was no need. Ms. Mattie had already pulled up the front door and was pulling us down the steps and into the car.

Grandmother's greeting was polite. "Good mornin', Mr. Edwards, how you this morning?"

Grandmother had known Mr. Edwards for years. She never mentioned how their friendship came to be, and Granddaddy did not seem to mind it. Mr. Edwards never came for visits. It was considered improper for an unmarried man to come visit a married woman unless he was very close to all the adults in the home, especially a husband and wife. Mr. Edwards wasn't.

He was an extremely large man with an unkempt shaven face. His eyes were deep-set, dark, and somewhat mysterious. Yet, he appeared to be a kind and gentle man. Whenever he spoke to us children, a smile eased across his unhandsome face. On the drive into town, he and Grandmother would hold conversations in which they sometimes disagreed with each other, but he never raised his voice or disrespected Ms. Mattie. Perhaps their years of friendship had endeared him to her as well as revealed to him that it would be futile for him to argue against her. Ms. Mattie had the ability to support her convictions in a disagreement and she did not have to raise her voice, either.

"Mornin' Ms. Mattie, I'm just fine, thank you. How's you girls this mornin'? Ms. Mattie, I declare they's growing like weeds. Must be all that good cookin' of yours." He laughed at himself as he rubbed his wide hand across his protruding abdomen. I could not help but wonder who was responsible for him growing like weeds around the middle.

"Well, Ms. Mattie, I see it's time for your trip to town. Seem like that's the only time I see you and these pretty little grandchildren of yours. You got a lot to pick up, do you?" He glanced with familiarity at my Grandmother but without smiling like he had done when he spoke to us.

"No. I don't need much. I won't be too long. I'm much obliged you comin'." Grandmother seemed to weigh out her words. She spoke but did not look in his direction. Instead, she adjusted her hat and looked out the window. The straw hat she usually wore when going to the cotton field had been replaced by her Sunday-go-to-meetin' hat as were the clothes and shoes.

Mr. Edwards turned the key to start the car as he spoke, "Well, now, we're all in here. I suppose we best get on the road. It'll take a while to get there and back. I don't wanna end up in town come dark." This time he did smile at Ms. Mattie at the end of his words. His words sounded more like a warning than a conversation.

Apparently, Grandmother understood. She nodded in his direction to indicate knowledge of his concern without his clearly saying it.

We settled in for the long drive to town, leaving the cotton fields and the glittering gravel behind. It was clear, as we drew nearer to town and farther from the country, that town was a much different place. The graveled road gradually shifted to smooth, paved streets. The shabby, framed farmhouses faded out of view and were remodeled into beautiful red brick homes with grass yards and some even with swings hanging off the tall trees. It looked like a different world had run up to meet our eyes. The farther we got from our house, the bigger the world seemed. Trees other than the familiar pine trees on the land where we lived accented the streets like silhouettes against the taller buildings in the distance.

Our country roads with few travelers were no match for the town streets with seemingly hundreds of people. Town was always crowded and people moved about without speaking to each other or even looking at one another. Instead they passed by with glazed-over eyes, trancelike.

Mr. Edwards brought the long dirty white car to a stop parallel to the sidewalk. Grandmother opened the door and we stepped out onto the hot pavement, "I'll be but a few minutes. I'll be lookin' for you right 'bout here." Grandmother smoothed her handmade flower-patterned dress, adjusted her rolled-up stockings and pulled us across the street to the stores.

She never lingered or engaged in conversation with the other women who had also come into town. My sister and I never lingered, either. These other women, diverse in complexion but still the same as Grandmother, seemed as hurried as Grandmother and held close any young 'uns they had with them.

Grandmother stepped with a hurriedness seldom seen when she was around the house. She selected a few items and was quickly finished. We took our direction from her and never asked for anything. She knew what she had come to buy and that was that.

When we stepped outside from the last store, the sun had risen higher in the sky and was beating heat down on our heads. The hat Grandmother wore shielded her eyes but not the heat. She searched for Mr. Edwards, but he had not returned. Rather reluctantly and almost with annoyance, Grandmother led us into an unfamiliar building. We had come to town at other times, but never had she taken us into this place. She walked a little slower as we entered the small building through the double-glassed doors. She stepped cautiously, as if time had changed for her and put her in a place she did not feel free to move about. We sat down, waiting for our ride to return.

Nesia and I did not dare talk or try to play. The heat of the sun had created a powerful thirst, but neither of us dared to ask Grandmother for a drink of water from any of the fountains. We were not old enough to read the signs posted above the two water fountains, but nothing in that room seemed to invite us to take a drink. Apparently, the long arm of Jim Crow had been able to reach into the city into that little place and with its finger pen words on a sign that would not allow my sister and me to feel comfortable to get a cool drink of water. So, we held our thirst in the same way Grandmother seemed to hold herself in her seat—reluctantly.

It seemed that the other women and children, much like us, had entered the same place in time. They too, sat quietly. Yet, others, whose flow of skin across their faces, arms, hands and legs were not butter brown, caramel, apple pie-yellow, or the color of dark red Alabama dirt, moved swiftly, talked loudly and with ease. Their children ran, laughed, giggled with each other and drank as much water as their stomachs could hold. We sat and waited, it seemed, for permission to move.

Grandmother followed an unspoken, but apparently, well-known and well-understood rule I had yet to learn. Obviously, the rule that applied to Ms. Mattie and others similar to her did not apply to those running children and loud-talking women; we did not belong and we were not to act as if we had a right to be there. Intense lines formed across Grandmother's forehead. The turned down corners of her mouth and the whiteness of her knuckles held tightly upon her lap was cause for concern. Grandmother may have understood and followed the unspoken rule, but she didn't like it. She kept her eye on us and on the outside. It was evident Mr. Edwards was not coming quickly enough for Grandmother. She was a patient woman even under the most extreme circumstances. But clearly, we were in a time and place beyond extreme.

Our ride appeared and Ms. Mattie gathered her pride and us and stepped out onto the street, opened the car door and got in. Grandmother did not speak of the moment and silence filled the car. The ride back to our house was not filled with the excitement it had going to town. Something unfamiliar to two little girls had happened, but familiar to Grandmother and to Mr. Edwards. Without her telling, he seemed to know. He knew enough to keep still. The car left the paved streets and eased onto the graveled road, welcoming as an old friend. Grandmother said, "Much obliged" to Mr. Edwards, turned, and walked into the house. Granddaddy had returned home and was seated in the front room with my brother. No words were spoken between Granddaddy and his wife, only a quick glance of acknowledgement. My brother lifted the weight of the grocery sacks from Grandmother's arms, mostly to see what she had bought since he did not go to town.

Grandmother was home again. It was clear she was back in her world. The lines across her forehead had faded back into her smooth skin. Her once white-knuckled hands were now preparing the evening meal. The food was good. The day was quickly coming to an end. Granddaddy left.

Grandmother did not require my sister and me to bathe in the Number Ten tub. Instead, she instructed all of us to get ready for bed. My brother found his way to his makeshift bed on the couch and tucked himself in. Nesia and I slipped underneath the covers on Grandmother's big bed and waited for sleep. Before I closed my eyes to wait for the morning, I saw Grandmother. She seemed tired, but not the kind of tired from working hard or having a busy day. Whatever happened behind those double-glassed doors in town wore heavy on Grandmother. It was a weight not as easily removed as my brother taking the grocery bags from her arms. It was shoulder weight, and she had carried it a long time. The trip into town was just a reminder it was still there.

Ms. Mattie's day came to an end. She knew she would recover from the trip, as she had done in the past and almost every day of her life in Alabama. But for now, as night drew in the stars and flung them against the sky, she lay down on her pallet on the floor and said goodnight to the sun.

The End of The Day

The years in Alabama with Grandmother seemed to have passed slowly, as time often does in childhood, but it wasn't nearly as long a time as it seemed. My sister, brother and I would not grow up into adulthood in Alabama as our parents had done. We would have no need to escape the cotton fields or the difficult work of the rural south. We would eventually leave Alabama to join Mother and our stepfather in Tennessee. Grandmother would also make the journey out of her Alabama south, only to return without her grandchildren. Her return would not last her life time. She would travel once again out of Alabama, but she would never return.

The day would come when Grandmother would stop getting up to wake up the sun and it would seem like hazy days ever since. I didn't know what it would be like the day Grandmother didn't get the sun up. Ms. Mattie had walked the country roads of Alabama most of her life. It was her road. Alabama was her South. It had bred generations of Ms. Mattie's kin and she had left it behind. Long before she left Granddaddy and Alabama, Granddaddy had left her for an alcohol mistress long before he died. It was his final call to rest that set her free from the sharecropper's house and the well across the road.

Finally, her children had come back to the cotton fields and picked up their mother. Ms. Mattie would watch the dust settle behind her for the last time. Her life would make a lot of turns and she would end up miles from where she had started and from where I had first known her. Her cotton fields would turn to fluffy white clouds floating above the New York skyline and her dusty graveled roads would curve into and collide with the paved streets of the busy city. She would take subway rides in place of mule-drawn wagons.

I would cease to watch Grandmother pack up her day's needs in her brown paper sack and ride away with her legs dangling off the back of the cotton pickers' wagon. Instead, from her apartment window in New York, as a young adult visiting her during my college spring break, I would watch her walk back from the grocery store to her three-room apartment, pulling a small but sufficient cart of groceries behind her, looking a little tired. Even that day, she had beaten the sun and me getting up and walked to the store.

Time would hold her there in the too-busy and complicated city of New York's tall skyscrapers, subways, and numbered blocks for only a while. Circumstances would find her on her way to a smaller, less complicated place, complete with a yard of grass, friendly neighbors, busy grandchildren, great grandchildren, and a front yard bench swing to pass away time. She would be nestled in the bluegrass of Kentucky and the warmth of her middle daughter's house; my Aunt Mae.

During my visits to Aunt Mae's, I would sit by Grandmother's side and slightly push our swing. I saw the accumulation of years, of change, of moving on her face. I saw a mother who had survived the death of two sons; her firstborn son at the early stage of her adult life and her lastborn son at the closing phase of her own life. I searched for a hint of sadness from a mother who had watched her middle daughter stand by the gravesides of three of her own children. Still, Grandmother seemed full of faith and hope. As I took into account the sum of the transitions in her lifetime, Ms. Mattie became even more so my strength.

The last time I left that swing, I thought nothing could happen in this world that could weaken her. She had made it weeping silently at the leaving of her parents, her grandparents, her two sons, three grandchildren, two husbands, and my father. I figured if Grandmother could survive all the dying and the moving, packing up and leaving the birthplace that she had lived in for over sixty years, and go to a place so contrary to all of her past living, nothing could bring her down. I was wrong.

Lynn was Ms. Mattie's firstborn grand-daughter and her heart. The day she died, it shook Grandmother's strength. Lynn left her only daughter without a mother and left her own mother without her only daughter. Three women, covering four generations, had lost a precious jewel from their crown and Grandmother would not be able to regain her full strength to move forward.

I wouldn't be there to see the light go out of Grandmother's eyes the day she heard her Lynn had taken her final journey, too soon and too fast. As time passed, Grandmother's strength weakened and gave way to a massive stroke. While I was miles away with time and distance between us, all of her strength would give out and my Grandmother would cease to wake up to wake the sun.

The phone call would come to Phoenix and I would rise to fly to Tennessee and find my way to Kentucky. My Grandmother was so much a part of me then and even more so a part of me now. In the quaint Kentucky chapel, I sat and waited for the preacher to stand and say things about a woman he never personally knew and to see some faces unfamiliar to me.

As I waited, I could not keep the flood of memories from spilling over. Transported back to the graveled roads of Alabama and Grandmother's sharecropper's house, I remembered the snow falling, cold, fast and hard, but inside the house was warmth. It was filled with the smell of coffee and burning wood. The black and white television blared out gunshots and resounding running hoofbeats as the westerns of *Gunsmoke* and *The Rifleman* etched out a dramatic storyline. In that same winter coldness, shut out by the warmth of the kitchen, I saw Grandmother with her hands full with raw meat from the hogs Granddaddy had slaughtered and was ready to grind into sausages.

I faintly recalled hot summers with surprising midday showers and mosquito-filled nights. Nights we gathered around the porch eating watermelon, fighting flies, and wiping eyes that had teared up because of the smoking barrel lit to chase the mosquitoes away. I remembered moments of laughter and complete quietness in the dark.

Ms. Mattie danced in my head to the rhythm that moved her as she hung the wash on the line or raised her hoe to chop another row of cotton. I smiled at the remembrance of her and some of her habits she had passed on to me. In that moment and in that small chapel, seeing her lying so quiet and still, I thought of her bed; big, soft, and covered over with her handmade quilts. I could hear her breathing from her pallet on the floor at the foot of her too-tall bed and wished I could stir her once more.

I was pulled back to the chapel from my travels through her life as I heard my introduction. I walked towards the front of the room and stepped onto the sacred platform, which placed me just above Grandmother and gave me a view of family. I saw the redness of her children's eyes, her grandchildren, and her great grandchildren. I saw my brother wipe tears away. I had known his love for our grandfather was great because he had needed him to be a father, but now, in this place, I saw his strong love for the woman who had always been there for him just as much as she had been for me and my sister.

I searched for words to ease our pain. My

voice gently rose to meet the silence and the challenge to sum up how her life had created the patchwork family that was now seated in that small Kentucky chapel. Although Ms. Mattie was so far from her Alabama home, as always, she was home in our hearts and we were there in her moment of honor.

I spoke only a moment, as her life and her imprint could not be fully summed up in the time allowed. The preacher picked up where I left off, lowering his voice as he spoke warmly of her. The air was still, but the silence almost overwhelming. When he had said his last, he called for those who would come and close Grandmother from my view forever. Draped in sadness and longing, her children, grandchildren, and great-grandchildren in procession with others stitched into the tapestry of her life, exited the chapel behind her. Even in death, Ms. Mattie led the way. We gathered our pain, crowded in a small succession of cars, and followed my Grandmother.

Patchwork Masterpiece

I followed the same route the hearse had taken the day before when it took away the woman who had wiped my nose, cleaned behind my ears in the Number Ten tub, and made sure I respected who she was. It brought her to the place only her body would be bound to stay. I had not cried the day she was lowered into the ground. In my reflective thoughts, I tried to sum up a life that couldn't be summed up in a lifetime. All of her years of living, and making the effort to shape my life, became the wind that carried me beyond the limitations of my existence and blew hope into my being. She was and I was because she was.

I found my way back to the place where she was laid. I sat in my car. Time drifted, seemingly without end, and I felt this can't be how it ends. Yet, it was. She was gone away and I was here missing her. I opened the door of my car and let my feet slip to the ground. With great effort, I lifted myself to a standing position. I turned to the left and walked around to the back of the car, leaning against it. I waited in deep, nearly unconscious thought. It is a long journey. I cast a glance at the mound that encased my strength. My heart cried, "How could this have happened? Who will wake Grandmother? Who will wake the sun?"

I stepped onto the soft earth and eased myself beside her. I tilted my head to watch an ant crawl over the carefully placed flowers. I reached across the mound and pulled a yellow carnation. I had to regain my own strength. I could only do that here, now and alone. My mind knew that she was not under that dirt, but my heart wanted to believe she was there, waiting for me to speak.

How could I fill the space with years of memories? Pails overflowing with plums picked one hot day and the plum jelly Grandmother had made, flooded my mind. The smell of freshly pulled peanuts lying on the front porch drifted past my senses. I saw Grandmother reaching into the stove and pulling out roasted peanuts. I saw her reflection in the looking glass as she swiftly passed by on her way to the kitchen, not even noticing that her pepper-gray hair was thinning. I heard her voice echo from the back door, "Suppertime." Sweeping past her echo and bringing three hungry children to the table, I caught the aroma of fried chicken, gravy, hot potatoes, cornbread buttered inside and out, and garden-grown, handpicked turnips and turnip greens.

From deep within I felt the motion of her movement as she rocked back and forth in the rocking chair. I heard her quietness as she listened to the rain falling on the tin roof of our little house. I felt the pull and lift of the comb as she made each stroke against my tangled hair. Her patchwork quilts formed a rainbow across the sky and I saw her hand carefully stitching each piece together; strong, yet gentle, but now silent hands. I refused to raise my hand to wipe away the tears that fell. And soon a flood followed and I wept for the memory of her. My soul longed to see her eyes and to hear her voice.

She had been my grandmother all of my life

and she was my home. She was the place I went when I needed to find myself. When the voice of God spoke so softly and clearly in my heart and I needed to remember where I first heard Him, Grandmother's little wooden framed house deep in the Alabama South was the point of my remembrance and my return. Only she was not there and the house wasn't there. All of my remembering couldn't bring that little house back, nor my Grandmother. In all of my pain of losing the place that grew me, in her I found what I believed in and the strength to live by it.

She was what she was and I could not believe that she would leave without saying goodbye. Silence rushed in and I realized she had already spoken. Of having pride, she spoke when she told me to hold my head up as we walked to church. She spoke of the oppression of injustice, yet the strength of silence gained only when you define who you are and not those seeking to be your oppressors. When the lines formed across her forehead while she sat in silence waiting for our ride to take us from town back to the gravel roads of the country and she never uttered a word of anger or discontent to those who surrounded her, she spoke of the importance of inner strength, quiet pride, and self-respect.

When she sat in the cotton pickers' wagon with her legs dangling off the back and her only leisure time was sleep time, Ms. Mattie was speaking of the reward of working hard and of hard work. She spoke of the necessity of finding what you believed in and keeping it intact despite hardships. Her hope and belief in her God was evident on Sunday mornings. Grandmother reveled in the power and deliverance of God's love in the church. The wooden floors would shift with the weight of feet pounding to the soulful rhythmic flow of the thunderous voice of a charismatic black preacher. Sunday church was always packed with people unloading their burdens and picking up their Bibles 'cause that was the only way they were going to go back to the cotton fields on Monday and keep pickin' cotton another week.

Ms. Mattie spoke of family love when she

placed the handmade biscuits on the table—the smell overflowing the tiny kitchen, spilling over into the front room and out through the broken screen door and across the cotton fields. In those cotton fields, when she willingly carried the weight of her grandchildren along with the heavy sacks stuffed with cotton bolls, Grandmother fulfilled her love of family and personified the essence of sacrifice. Grandmother's ability to give up the gravel roads of Alabama for the paved city streets of New York and Kentucky spoke of the necessity of being flexible to change. Life had taught her to accept that there are some things you can't change, but there are times when some things will change you. She had taught me, by her life, to change the way I handled some things and to change my thinking on the way some things handled me.

Grandmother's living was a silhouette of Langston Hughes' poetic lyric, "Life for me ain't been no crystal stair..." There were times she had found life difficult to live, but found sitting down even harder. She was a revolution in the making, refusing, by the strength of her silence, to bow to the definitions of others to define her. She echoed the sentiments of Malcom X's infamous phrase, "By any means necessary" by staying true to who God had designed her to be in spite of circumstances surrounding her and people trying to make her less than what she was. She did whatever she had to do. Ms. Mattie chose to work in the hot, often dusty and sometimes snake-filled cotton fields, instead of the white man's house; refusing to clean a house she could not live in, wash clothes she could not wear, cook food she could not eat or raise children she had not borne.

Grandmother experienced Martin Luther King, Jr's inspiring prophetic eulogistic deliverance, "I've been to the mountaintop and I've looked over, and I've seen the Promised Land" when she closed her eyes and never opened them in this world again.

I sat beside her mountaintop and heard her last and lifting words of letting go. I realized she spoke of letting go, when, in that small, yet busy front yard at Aunt Mae's house in Kentucky, she sat on the swing and let me gently push. Now, it was my time to let go. It was more difficult than I thought it would be. I had known the time was coming for her going, but I had not known the pain her leaving would bring. Her life had been long lived. Her time had been well spent and her words spoken well. There was nothing left to say. Her life echoed her wisdom and her wisdom etched her life.

I gathered my memories, my sadness, my pain, my strength, and walked back to my car, opened the door, and sat down. I raised my head, only to look in the mirror and see her looking back in my eyes, the outline of my face and the shape of my lips. She had not birthed me, but she had borne me. For years of making me what I was to be, Grandmother took the weight and carried it. She carried it on the hot, dusty, gravel roads into the cotton fields and back home at the close of the day. The weight of the responsibility of shaping a life she held tightly in her hands, with the same hands used to stir the batter of the cornbread and place it inside the wood-burning stove. In her heart, Ms. Mattie held me and for all of the years of knowing her, now, my heart was full of her.

Grandmother will always be my strength, even in death. In the rearview mirror, I looked back at her looking at me. I turned my head toward the road that led out of the place that held her. What else could I do? Mattie, a patchwork masterpiece, was now covered in eternal peace. There would be no need to wake her to wake the sun. It had set, as it had done all those years, and it would rise, as it had done all those years, without Grandmother.

About the Author

Nelby A. Littleton is an ordained minister, writer, artist, and mother of two adult children. Reverend Littleton was born in her mother's house in the rural south of Alabama. She is the youngest of 3 children. She and her two older siblings spent their formative years in the sharecropper home of her grandmother and step-grandfather before moving to Nashville, Tennessee to live with their mother and step-father.

During her high school years, she developed a passion for all things art related. She was a commercial art's major at Austin Peay State University in Clarksville, Tennessee with a passion for creating works of art. She had not yet discovered her love of the written word.

In 1983, Reverend Littleton accepted the call to ministry and was the first female licensed by the Late Bishop Michael Lee Graves, Founder and Pastor of the Temple Church in Nashville, Tennessee. As a result of her ministry, she received the Who's Who Among Women Award. In 1985, Reverend Littleton served as a writer for the Women's Foreign Missionary Guide. A desire to strengthen her skills to effectively minister to the needs of others, Reverend Littleton moved to Dallas, Texas to attend Dallas Baptist University with a major in psychology and remained in Dallas after graduation. It was there she found her passion for the written word and began the journey of sharpening her natural skills of communication and a flare for the use of profoundly descriptive words and phrases. Reverend Littleton developed a gift of visualizing things in an extraordinary way and articulating her vision on paper. Mattie: A Patchwork Masterpiece was born out of that ability.

Reverend Littleton continues to write to inspire others; including a book of poetry entitled Suddenly Love as well as other works currently in progress which she endeavors to have on the shelves for her readers.

9 780998 289267